NIGHT TRANSIT

Also by P. R. Anderson

Poetry Collections

Litany Bird (Carapace, 2000)

Foundling's Island
(Electric Book Works: UCT Writers Series, 2007
and uHlanga, 2018)

In a Free State: A Music (uHlanga, 2018)

NIGHT TRANSIT

P. R. ANDERSON

Poems

DRYAD PRESS

People! Read Poetry

Night Transit

Dryad Press (Pty) Ltd
Postnet Suite 281, Private Bag X16, Constantia, 7848,
Cape Town, South Africa
www.dryadpress.co.za/business@dryadpress.co.za

Cover design & typography: Stephen Symons
Copy Editor: Helena Janisch
Front Cover Image: *Die Hart van Dagbreek* (2021) by Hanien Conradie,
ochre on canvas 115cm x 85cm
Back Cover Image: *Tankwa Dawn* (2021) by Hanien Conradie,
ochre on canvas 115cm x 85cm
Inside Images: *Die Groot Verlange* (2021) and *Silence Behind the Sound* (2021)
by Hanien Conradie, soot ink on paper, 59.4cm x 42cm
Set in 9.5/14pt Palatino Linotype

First published in Cape Town by Dryad Press (Pty) Ltd, 2023

ISBN 978-1-991209-15-3 (Print)
ISBN 978-1-991209-16-0 (Electronic)

Visit www.dryadpress.co.za to read more about all our books and to buy them.
You will also find features, links to author interviews and news of author
events. Follow our social media platforms on Instagram and Facebook
to be the first to hear about our new releases.

for Mara Boccaccio

CONTENTS

3

4

5

1

The Folded Lake

The poet says *Come to the window*. Turn
your head: the rain is depending from a skyful

of seawater, ripping in the gusts of landfall,
knocking down the coral flowers, soaking

the dumped ash of a long winter. It is so
beautiful. Through the cloud, the great ships

moan like whales, and the cloud stinks of fish.
Winter that will not yield. If you like, we can chase

curfew and get to the granite and strip
to swim in the surge, drive home in the heat

of the car, complicit, sad and alive, choosing
our music, which may be the only thing to do.

Spring that is late has put out plum blossom
like popcorn, and the mountains shine back

at it their unseasonal ice. We have bread to tear
that the prior earth has yielded in its array

of wheat, where the cranes dance. To say
we are speechless is to say we are staggered

at what has to be said, that we have seen
what our hand has done. We are beseeched

in the bowels of Christ to think we may be
wrong, as we are. Wrong as the world is, that is

lovelier than rain on an iron roof, waking us
to consciousness again, of our salt skin.

I dreamed I took a lake out of its valley,
folded it over my arm and traversed a range

more home than ever home was. How many
suns were sunk there? Come to the window:

there is all the world we know, and all we care
to know. Help me shake out the lake again.

First Light

Surely you will know it: somewhere beyond
the last cold city lights, the last of that
small-hour transit air: sweet milk, myrrh, the dung
of standing cattle, a wind-farm milling
the least shift of it under garnet lights.

That's where you pull over to fill the tank,
empty bladder, stamp feet on the concrete
of an oily forecourt, where the muzak
miscarries on cold air. Cheerful coma.
So many hours out, you find your mind hangs.

You're stuck in two-thirds of a precious thought
wrought to the pitch of music, singing you
almost aloud. You have to stop the engine
in your shook cells, ringing skin, and then look
out from the halogen day to total

night without. You see there this rind of blood,
thin as a theory of conflagration,
some impossible seam of carbon's own
kiln fired of itself under its own weight,
and every critic in you screams *Lush! Lush!*

Romantic guff! The thing is, it hangs there,
same as the meaty fumes of fuel, the tract
of phatic Xhosa at the pump, money,
the Coke your hung mind pleases at, the bin
you bung it in. Enduring lateral

lightning, the crush of smelter coke. All hope
of making sense of things combusted, you
will climb back into your ton of doubtful
sovereignty and bowl on at however
many rpm. Day will come as detail,

as finches, their handful of gravel flung,
as dreary kilometres, as cattle
knee-deep in the porridge of the landfill
somewhere, and forgetting your small Xhosa
for this long sigh in English, myrrh and dung

indeed. It's not that you've anything much
to say, milling your breath for its dividend
of the purportive real, something to hope
of a gust of finches, a can of Coke,
the red peel of a sunrise, poetry

slapping in your heart's bilge till it gasps out
the usual noises: yes, people suffer,
yes, the dorps hang on under the spires, strewn
with crematorial grit, shitloads of rubble,
yes, sparrows fall, crows prosper, and who cares?

Will you know this, or do you still? Perhaps
that is really what the eastern fissure
insists. That there be some things sufficient
of common quandary, intense enough
to look at in any language and make

this mess of. Let's say of the travelled heart.
It's no manifesto, but of some kind
of history, of being as that bag-man you
saw rummaging in the first light, who lugged
the same stuff, tipped it all out, put it back.

Origin

It differed by a dawn, the next day, the day
offering *next* to be known. It seemed forever
I was on a void water, thumping the mass

of it like a great door to be entered, but
the dark disrupted me and nothing passed
for a password, say, so I chugged

without chug succeeding chug, and the depths
heard nothing. Then the flotsam of the first
dawn, the whole dictionary: out of the hitherto

dark the sea took plasma, whipworms
on fire, and the swell began as downs under
skin of dorado. I would say I was

assailed, seeing the sail put from the rising
air, birds carving out leagues, and the ready
water spread with a spermaceti of light.

*

All that had been turned out to be past,
the striving. I could remember now. I made
land out of no direction but where it lay,

coming slowly there by the tubbing stroke,
smuts of the exhaust cast on the water, no
more than a guess of ash put to the Ganges.

I went up into the prow and I said
to the mud tide, *Receive me and you
will be fertile to the fact*. The waters took

breath of the boat away, and the birds
towed me the last part possible. I jumped
ship of that void vessel for a silt shore,

seeing green like a parrot for the first time.
Landfall was the multiples of light; my body
foundered on the good coast of its skin.

                         *

Three ages I sat on a scrub dune righting
my eyes that were not readily believed.
Middens of oyster rose, suns rummaged

the pearl of them. I shucked the days, I burned
the middens for a lime kiln, dressed
myself stone, made a feather god. I invented

splendour and kept to myself.
I came to be a people before me,
throng of the aforegone, whose sepulchral

middens I reverenced in the evening heat.
I held the hinterland equally,
yesterday and tomorrow, I remembered

what I was going to do, and by signs
said so to the sand that the sea stole over.
And over again wrote the sun down.

*

I shook another from the sand, a sand-wife,
scaffolded of bones brought to light,
who said *These words become me,*

I shall be the mother of pearl. I washed
her at the sand well, careful not
to sink us in the quick of it. I hung on her

drilled cornelian that the sea found me
like trouble. She said *I was before*
you, waiting at these prior bones, this shore

settled on you. I saw that it was true
to the bone, and as the day is long and over.
The next day we had forgotten

our sovereignties in a sea change, falling
into step, fettered at the shadow, in the foam
where we trod the sea back to itself.

*

Out of their green bunks the small apes broke
like a wave to my middens and would not
answer to their names. I heard my head

preach *Teach them*, and for good I raised a fist
at their sea mist, and a stone to them
on my only land. So catechised the dead.

The monkey clambered through its own
burned blood to the branches. The stars
took up a version, and then a novel dawn,

ash cantering before the wind back
to its dark trees. I had cremated worlds,
made physics, populated gods.

I fetched the first stone and I knew
for certain what the moon was made of, that
the moon was what the sun threw.

*

So we came inland by the stars' names
put like telegraph through our reckoning
fingers. We stole upriver and the water

shone with stars, the lights of possible cities.
We mended punctures. The hills came
into mountains to be passed like days

of snow, where we left our spent oxygen.
We had grown gravid with beginning
bibles, and to remember Ur

was our far wandering, and more to suffer
than an oncoming Sahara, the flies
there and the varieties of tomorrow.

We learned the wheel from the stars.
We became a people satellites might see,
melted things down, took blood seriously.

*

On what farther shore I set down I know
not, but that I have closed this great door
as doors ask of their being. There is still

a source, clear water speaking its half
of questions put to it, taking us in hand.
The middens are raked. No apes but us

regarding the tall sea, daybreak and nightfall.
Behind me our ossuaries assemble
an army that stops at nothing. I begin

to begin again their ageless afterward.
Let be, stars and the modalities
of blue, the green rind of my first jungle come

back to a happenstance I lived to sunder.
With a sharpened spoon I dig out the channel
in the bone and I eat its sea.

*

Rain comes as a bride broken free to light,
sliding to the sea, wrapping the forest, it turns
children to aeroplanes, it falls

as sugar at the wedding. Invisibly far,
mountains are siphoning wet air up their passes,
radio splinters like a sawn tree, soused lungs

of light gasp. There have remained
these common minutes, more than agreed,
when the polity is washed as I first washed it

at the quick source, careful of absorption.
The sea fills. The great birds are roused
in hives of light. The leaves make morse.

Nothing is saved, but let get wet, and I,
who remember no womb, guess at the brack
cataracts drawn down land of me away.

The Coming Poem

Gravid at dawn, at dusk, but fast
asleep. You have yet no name nor
will declare yourself. I could number you
One. And so I do.

Always there is this parturition biding.
What I want is voice, must do
with your harking on, the loud
nick in the vinyl going round:

so far you are a dolphin
and we have begun. I turn to books.
I find in Thomas Browne a page
on thunderstones.

I issue you this passport then, that you
might travel where we may not. Come:
home is the hunter with his hare
by the ears. Tell us what we ought.

A Full Confession

When I grew to about thirteen years of age . . . I was contrited
under a sense of power and love.
– Sarah Lynes Grubb, 1832

Even in this life we have more than one.
I knew it on frontier roads, years past
knowing, in the rear-view, which is a mirror
true only to our always leaving now:

a cast-iron gate, a farm, divided ground
garrisoned with aloes, their staves of fire.
I drove away, as down the dwindling coral
avenue, drove down a backward glance

where all my selves were shed as the spent rust
skins of flowers, tinder under the wheels,
thorns, and clay-stone gravel, the gathered dust
settling on us under the common law.

Yet knew the place, and what of it, this redoubt
on blood ground, a place of shouts and small war,
fire seething in thicket, of burred goats, night
puttering in the generator, and filled

with whistles out of the third polity
bristling in resumption every dark.
Do not forgive me that I was there once
glorified; nothing was less simple then.

Strange, but I cannot complicate you now.
Recall the thrilled dogs nipping the air, cold,
reserved sunlight in winter, and the waiting
on whistles doodling out of sight, and wives

in nylon and on nylon folding chairs,
and then the barrage of .303s,
ordnance docking scuts of soil, the horned ram
ploughing it up to his kneeling elbows.

And who was praying to whom? A carcass,
later, on the flatbed. Night falling like soot,
handfuls of hot samp, your samp eyes, drifting
mawkish to the iron barn to kiss until

your knees shook. Could we hold in common arms
one country of vicious grace, the quiet ram,
somewhere impossible, of a samp manna?
What faith on false ground? I grieve, grieve it all.

2

That Other Country

She comes into it crossing rain
crossing itself in worried air, worrying down.
She crosses the arable. Clay
takes her shoes, as she had for granted.
There is a way of seeing the weather
shawl her, rain fall to her, out where
she stoops on the edgeless watershed.
Any way you go's away. *Item,*
figure, grey, in a country of.
You wonder exactly where
the birds go not to drown, as also
where the spade is ringing, not,
strangely, where she's going.

Years later, many as the countries
between, her stockings
that day ladder my heart to remember:
mud on a teal nylon.
It could be her ankles were smashed.
Because this was in the Odeon
under the balconies of my ribs, there
was a suitcase spilled in the ploughland,
of course. What do people
take with them into history, love,
the risky heartlands? Knickers.
Sardines. A change of clothes,
that's the thing.

And who was digging in that weather
of wet ash, flurries, field
after field, and where? She let me
tie her together with twine lashed
under the handle at the clasp.
This could have been in Poland, she
bereft. Poland, ploughland,
she clasped my hand. Only *Poland*
stands for a standing rain that aches, the sound
there of a spade ringing in rain.
Who's digging the rain? She came
in out of it, guttering, just
in time, as they closed the borders.

Delta

Months have passed, each one filled with foreboding and silence.
Now disasters are flowing together into a delta that has no name,
and will only be given one by geographers, who will come later,
much later.
– John Berger

Many years on the water, many
generations.
Something more massive than a
mood, waking

in the wake of a dream. He makes
the shore of day,
leaves a net of light lying in his
shallows, lymph.

Gets up. Getting hot. His muds, his
pharaonic
plovers. Snow he can only imagine,
but falling.

Daughters are half water. Long after
dark, water
passes in their eyes. He works for
Delta Soda.

Pride is the man set up on his
bicycle, to work,
pedalling out of the dream in a
controlled fall

forward into the reeds, gasping at the catching
of the light. Birds, their handbells
there.

So should snow fall on these oldest diligences,
the husbandry of mud, the drowning
bells. Afar,

old words are tweezered, and the annual cloud
guts itself on Ruwenzori. Into
oncoming cotton

he pushes, under a black Rosetta
slab. No dream
should confuse his bones with the
heat of bicycle

steel, but birds knuckle the spokes
now, and his girls'
eyes have whitened and desisted. He
puts out a hand

as a man landing a boat puts out a
hand, but he can't
outreach the unfathomable winter of
the dream;

his daughters' eyes thaw with tears,
birds go
to ground, and the river is turning
soda at his touch.

Heinz Guderian at Yasnaya Polyana

Fahrkarte bis zur Endstation

You come all this way in a shirtsleeves war,
the white dust of it ground out of a white sky,
and it's such good going, you feel the cause must be.

A panzer is a creature of anticipation;
it knows, because it is, what will happen next.

Were we caught short or too far out?
It's an artilleryman's question. We were out
cold. The vacuum tubes burst in our radios.

Winter, the white flag of the latitude.
As the poet says, *we are all held in a single honour.*

This is how war is made on war that is
otherwise always with us, until hell itself
freezes over. At Yasnaya Polyana

I allowed art to be burned for scrap heat.
The year had laid a lead white on white cloth.

Allow me this observation of frame and canvas:
that the fire is in the wood. We live late
in the world to think that we set fire. Fire's found.

So the ice at Yasnaya Polyana came out of the ground
and found me out, who had bestrode a summer

of a thousand miles with kaolin in my hair, my goggles,
and the sun itself watched and shone to me,
the warrior who took the horse out of war.

There we had to lay up in the mercy of the next
to happen, which was us, because we were.

Yasnaya Polyana was the last station. In the end,
it was a spiritual problem, a white conclusion
I drew there, but not because it was where

he wrote of war and peace, and the tale of Karenin's wife.
I began that, like this campaign, and I do

know this: that as she settles in the train, fretting
in fever, sweating the oil of battle,
the carriage window fogged, turret sight lost,

that she is in, and what trouble.
I know it because I felt the same,

writing to Gretel from Yasnaya Polyana, writing
of how the last exhaustion was not physical
but spiritual. I felt the same, that I was in, and how deeply

snowed in, writing with inks of frostbite and gangrene,
that the end of art was scant thermal energy,

my turret sight was lost, and it would all end
badly, between the tracks and the train.
A tank is a train that lays its own tracks forever.

In the midst

of the too few alienable dawns, the kind
to be prised from the fact of day and set
aside, filed between the third and fourth ribs,
because in a strange city, otherly belled,
whose light is rapturously dismal, a smut
with dusk begun in it, plainly historical,
in the sense of belonging to an unknown
story, off by heart to you and yours, its own
late risers, who see not the light but by it,

I have taken up Belgium, like smoking.
It was wet verdigris, a seep cloud, the *eglise*
tolling through 360 degrees. Somewhere
in the building, contraptions of ascension.
That was the first blood in the lavatory.
That was the day our daughter quickened.
Everything was below the belt. I adore
Brussels to this day, where we grew two
tumours, spoke on the pillow, slept more.

Potato Fields

Her death keeps seeming to me
light levelling on potato fields—not so
very strange: almost the home farm

at homing, gilded, there
the terrible leaves
cooling, their proffered hearts,

just shifting in the air,
got going between the buried
heat and the dying day.

Why do I look that way?
Who would not put their face to the balm
of a merciful west,

turn away from what goes on
and on, the rags of television flown
over fields, the loping

signal thronging the cable?
Behind is what lies ahead, the wreck
in the yard, slowly crashing

into itself, its half-acre next
to the potato fields. I see
the mashed fill of her sleeping-bag

strewn on the tar
and her sleeping forever.
The field is lit for that.

The Goldfinch Variations

1. *Carduelis carduelis* (*Fringilla carduelis*. Linn. 1758)

Dawn on the Palatine:
planets bow out, stars pick their way
through rat-traps and incident tape.
The morning after the party of all time.

The sun loves me like a cat
wanting my sleep. I am trying to sleep
in the lee of a wall in the wilderness
backyard of an emperor.

There is a lyric of ruins. It is a song
sung in that dream of eating your own teeth.
Red brick turns its flank to the sun.
bax bunny tattooed there.

Scudding across tufa and tramlines,
glittering like straights,
goes just the one scooter.
Ciao, bella.

This letter comes by goldfinch,
the first I ever saw,
blooding its face on the Palatine
at dawn, terrible

as a princeps, pontifex, come
down into gardens of citrus and cypress
in the first heat of the day.
A blood god busy in the cardoons.

2. Coleridge, Rome, Spring 1806

Though thou clothest thyself with crimson, though thou deckest thee with ornaments of gold, though thou rentest thy face with painting, in vain shalt thou make thyself fair: thy lovers will despise thee, they will seek thy life.
— Jeremiah 4: 30

Sparklings countless on the Leaves
of olive Trees after Rain;
woods peopled with Primrose Knots;
snow on Almonds oversnowed.

Memoir of Olevano,
yet idle if no inward
Spark lurks there, lurks unkindled.
Such a Spark, O man! A spark!

O Roman in the market,
twisting necks, chit-chatting there,
200 finches flutter
from your hands, 200 gold

finches gasping. Both your hands
thrown out in Oratory —
complicit. Is this a Poem?
Baffled finches, baffled flame.

Earth supply the fuel, heaven
the dry light air, themselves shall
make the current that will fan
& spread them. & all their force is vain.

3. On the Beaks of Finches

That, after all, they should serve
a doctrine of signatures,
begotten not made. They point
to the world they intend
to find, yet chisel it too.

As signs do, they show
us that signs do
more than show. Got, they beget.
This is why the pro's won't
kiss when it comes to it:

the sign swallows its own lie,
becomes the thing. Making out
makes a world. So a child
kisses the mirror, because a child
puts everything in its mouth.

Our purpose theirs,
to survive the unstoppable
accident of being. The sparrow
greets Lesbia with its beak.
Catullus gave her a verb, *to kiss*,

and a dead finch.
Words point at what they thresh.
So if we extrude a spine
for a beak because we live
among thorns on islands,

happenstance is happiness.
Our desiderata tend
to a wavelength underneath
the defences of cacti.
Accommodate. If what we do

is simulate the exo-
diacritic of the one
insect we prefer to eat,
should we be wholly surprised?
This was what we are after.

4. Casa d'Orazio, Roccagiovine

Remind us: the welder's hose of damp fire,
the sleeve of sparks worn where a chisel's ground.

They chase themselves through some far other day
high over the recycling bins, the tar

panhandle where the one bus burns an hour,
to decorate the tall fir at the shrine

of San Pio painted bronze, whose plastic flowers
fail like the real. Scarred with a sergeant's gold,

they fold in the dark needles. Flakes of light,
then gone. *Spores of mistletoe. Suds of ash.*

Who grinds out their accidental spark,
laying what chisel to what wheel? What torch

cuts their share of its blue daylight, welds us
to the pavement that they escape? You tread

the planet round and then you write them down
in faithless ink and find yourself in hope

of striking sparks. You find that you are watched
at that same window on which you both depend:

now eavesdropped there, it discovers you gold
— *Apollo's tiny eagle landed.*

Coda

And of that red regard? Only the probable
origin of all signs, all signature —
the trauma of platonic ink, so potent
it needs no alphabet to state what once
written is still read: *being's emergency.*

5. *The Nativity*

486 have been counted attending crucifixions,
nativities, annunciations, lighting from gallery to
gallery with the looping determination of phone-
lines seen in a car window or a train's. Or perhaps
they pass us over, flying through the night. In all
the mostly gilded windows, they congregate:
insignificant ambassadors of, or to, or from, the
significant event. To each treaty they bring their
blood seal, the daub, the oath. But the best are in
the best picture in the world. Piero has them fallen

by the wayside; you need to be a Samaritan to see them. They will not perch as Joseph on a saddle, nor lurk as the prescient magpie, and when the time comes they will not festoon the spar of judicial murder, nor pink the *lacrimae dolorosae* with their real presence. They will fossick the weeds. Blood runs on; that is the whole point, and when it falls, it falls to earth, incarnadine, to rust there in the dust where iron began. (And if you had to choose the god begun or the finches carrying on? It's not the sign of blood, but just the blood shed, the shed the god's born in, and the weeds that grow without.) Theirs is another picture, and the man whom they say was led blind through Sansepolcro at the end sees them as uncertainly as we do. You have to choose to see them either as they are or for what: what sheds your inward tears of you, brought to the light, the pitch of silence, the whole screaming, eternal morning, is not the choir's precise note, the Madonna so translated she looks unhuman, the levitating child, or Judea toppling into Italian perspective, but the gap into which your eyes fail, travelling from God to finch, with some relief, and back again.

What Went Down

Do you like Indian food?
Let's take a picnic to the cemetery;
what is our life but a picnic among its bones?
I was captured so courteously I forget the date.

Arm's length is the radius of responsible action.
I don't drink, but let me fill your glass
with wine the colour mostly of itself.
Do please forgive me, put your sleeve to my mouth.

Thank you, and for being here with the long
late light in your hair, your hair snagged in your
mouth, and you spitting it out like wine.
Your hair the colour of wine in fact.

Do you still like Indian food?
This is so-so, but I treasure now the blood-let
tandoori on my cheek, as if I put
up a fight. I was captured at the yew right here.

Let's walk past the bins out into the million
streets, our footfall the bells of foreign cities.
We are photographed together in the foil's flash,
stuffing the urn with buckled punnets.

Did you like the food, really?
It's a messy business; how much I like your
mouth and you murmuring wine there. Tell you what:
let's pretend we're dead, and just be walking.

The Photograph He Kept

Driven by desire to desire longing, for want
he kept her photograph against the odds
of time, and changing houses, for where she had

signed it with light and salts, shown her
particular constellation of bones, bending
naked for a fallen book. They read no more.

It was not then he kept, but the memory
itself, the glare of the flash setting
like a winter sun in the bay window, books

falling further into disarray every time
she stooped for them. Most of all, she paled
into significance, becoming less

and less the body he once held, held down
like a job, and was beholden to, but all
that memory can ever hold, something

tending to soul, of bones blown,
evacuated by years and years of radiation.
Every year he whitewashed them again.

Every year he saw less of her, but the stars
pricking out her joints, and the dark
vacancies for which he had first applied.

A Companion to Owls

1

It is the same owl that eludes
us, crouched in grass in bowered wings,
harrowing the high field, or sudden
immemorial on the sooted column.

Flies at dusk. But you have seen with day's eyes
(and the larks lift from all quarters)
her bouncing over marsh on a dry day
(crabs beetling like telegraph),

taking her photographs. That once, she
exploded underfoot, a stealth drone.
Payload of tapped poppy.
Hush-hush.

2

All night, the demon
invective of the owl graving
curses. Its white rumour bulges
where termites climb
to the light in convoys.

& dawn:
cuneiform of its tattoo
trod in the dewed grit.

Pierrot sleeps. A litter
of takeaway poultry
bones, greasepaint, sherry bottles,
false nails. The drone ants
have died for their average. We
have woken now
and then to the exemplary.

3

Modern owls.
An essay.

There's a rogue in the suburbs,
a wisdom on fishponds.
The gilt koi are disposed
as a wrack of flowers the storm strew
in your sleep. You heard nothing.

& sentinel over the rush-hour
traffic on a cobra lamp, as the goddess does,
she knows you backward.

Minerva's business. To the high satellites
reporting, that roll the world. Under there
the mathematics of shot-silk seas, corals
of debouching waters, the shingles of cities.

4

You could go off the edge like a knife.

Owl is a cough it only has to.

& worlds on worlds on its x-ray shown.

& stoops like lungs on a breathless moment.

Wild Duck in the Marshes

Tell el-Amarna, New Kingdom

Over millennia it keeps its stalled faith
with the real, backstroking in ascent
over the lotus confronting it, put up

out of the hiding bulrushes, treasure.
Its pinions are spread to the ongoing air,
its gut tucked, breast given in the exact

attitude of duck bone. Goethe says
blue has no need of it, being the theory
of itself precisely. You could say

here it strives for faience, but nature
resumes it, a river blue. The paint
merchants would style it *Blue Nile*.

A duck rising in accurate light, on the far
side of morning or evening. Across
the negligible ages you hear the whurry

of wings and forsaken water, the bronze
alarm hacking the air, and smell the silt
nethers of rush root and lotus. But look

again and you will see everything drawn
to itself in a doctrine of signatures:
the spread wedge of its tail reports

to the committee of lotus, and each
fan of the peacock plant is a webbed foot.
The lotus is leaping up, and the rushes

feather the disturbing air, and the blue
hood of the duck is daubed for a river god
resurrecting, a blue sun over the marshes.

Whale Sharks, Mozambique Channel

Everyone dreams of a dugong
grazing under their elected dhow,
a Buddha in Indian seagrass, and to talk it

up like a sermon, with a fire built
on sand in the hull, the night
sky quarrying its stars there in the flue.

But the dugongs have gone. Somewhere
they hold council with the coelacanth
under atolls, in languages that will die too.

Argonauted in neoprene,
to take the water, warm as urine. A smutter
of exhaust blows on the channel.

This is a creation to lower the eyes.
Roar of the soundless undersea, of coursing
blood and plugged air in the ear,

the screed of the 3-D steppes of plankton
shinnying like sperm in their migrations,
whole weathers bowled

over there, as if
in a *National Geographic* film. Dolphins
dote with their fixed rubber grins.

And sailing so massive, they are truly sudden
in the twilight: these panzer sharks,
webbinged with glyphs

—dalmatian, solitaire—
going south in this paintwater sea …
Unfathomable hope

to see through this rumorous now
the integrity of a planet, just-
just perceptibly drifting down there: the platonic

ovum, the milk-blue principle, the shark
crêped in clouds,
liver-spotted, life-lined.

Insects

that are the language of nights and high noons
and the signature of silence too—consider only
the lateral snow of migrating whites, erratic

but moving north across the farm, and the dead
quiet of the ferrymen walking against water
on hot days while the grass screams under

its breath, or erupts underfoot. These you
take too for granted, as that invisible biomass
fidgeting at the edge of rational concerns and

the human compass, now past negligent, the smudge
on the windscreen, that pus streak of abdomen
burst on the glass and writing something not

more than itself, never as clever as *thorax* or
arthropod. But while the radiator ticked
in some scorched shade, you used to admire

the torn and the crucified, the harvest there
of your industrial shrike, its mowing the air
that is now simplified of small things, wings

which by night bore to the light caught
in the hissing mantle, and battered the glass
there for their share of the same grace as held you

encompassed and illumined, in which
you saved face, and read the writing you cared to,
and thought nothing of the shadows

cast by that preposterous love, so surely
blinding, that blew in your hair like the light's own
air got up, as in the wicks of Pentecost.

Deposition of Marsyas

1. Because the hegemonic of the world
is man, so I was upperwise a man,
but goat below, for earth's asperity.
2. The book says so. 3. My music cut both ways.
4. It hurt but God it was so beautiful.
5. Music is all that cuts both ways, is all.
6. No god can get it but by drawing breath.
7. I took her philosophic breath away
and only what she never had to lose.
8. I made those reeds sing like bones the absence
of their marrow. 9. I drew blood till you wept.
10. I drew the note of blood out of this world.
11. Apollo made a lyre of me always.
12. No god can get it but by living death.

Pan

God of the flocks, meaning roughly
    mayhem, we brake at pace for this your
ecumenical sign, the red rag flown
    on a herd's stick held wide, chivvying
dust and the rarest light, winter
    at altitude, to sit in the stunned air
under the window, radio playing. You
    pass through as the flock topples
across ditch and dust, whistled up,
    summoned in that pandemic tongue,
hoi hoi, yup yup, ish ish, and by men
    with hats and pipes, in jackets plucked
by a thief wind, a poplin of sheepfat.
    The college of your priests can
whittle a shank of its meat, grout
    out its last marrow, in a minute. You
know their knives, whet to a fin of steel.
    Deft they are and vested in dust
to the knees, in long lanolin gloves,
    their liturgy is whistled, and their prayer
is counted, and they never fall asleep
    telling the hundreds or at noon, when to do
so is to court your horror: havoc
    brought as knives walking among the lambs.

Under the Eye

I grieve the entoptic
creatures that were once more
in my waters. I had
only to close my eyes.

Dugongs of the mind's eye.
They grazed on retinal
seagrass, they dredged in sills
my sands, my shaken globe.

The sun would stain them red
in a harvest water. Now
harpooned; their water-downs
are gone to dunes, their runes

unread go unresolved.
An occasional dhow
drops sail and a sighting
spreads its rumour like ink:

neuronal deltas flow
after far storms, algal
continents multiply,
reagents stain again.

I see what Webb and Hubble send,
lava fires, plasma wells,
blisters of apple bile,
slow gentian tinctures, lewd

nebular congresses,
conjugal cells, and what
else goes on like kissing
inside-out. Stigmata

prove me, and prove by this
the witness of the skin.
This is our first eye and
how the world looks within.

Umnyele

~ *for KF*

The stars as facts, not things,
and facts a range of rumour:
is—or was—Aldebaran
as lovely as its name?

Still—almost—that great hail
of light, those hackles raised
over us, the issue:
the far past's brilliant now.

Light years between us, let
each our perfected past
find present here, and stars in one
joint instant understand.

The Other Stars

The other stars. And how I must lean back
into alteration. The conjunct planets and the familiar
Sisters turn me out like a pocket. There's the west.
I steer north by certain ignorance. They seem

so few, a poor haul. And there's the groundshine
of Milan. Long after sunset its umbrous flare.
A blue light wheedles through the candle trucks,
intrudes its wavelength in the spectrogram

of tail-lights, indicators, brakes: the blushing
night elected in the beams. Is it the plague?
How every country has its own tune, ambient
of days and films. Is it the plague?

Glad that the daughters got away as doves.
My bull cartwheels on Aldebaran.

Take Art (Burning the Pictures)

*O ye religious, discountenance every one among you who shall
pretend to despise Art and Science!*
—William Blake

(Behind glass)

Kristallnacht. Who'd not hoped to exercise
his radius in a private dust, where now
all's silicate? He feels so far away.
A kite of ibises trails over trains.

(Human rites: art surgery)

Blown lotus of the uncooped ribs, and time's
sawbones stooped over the coxcombed city: there
the live abraxas, legged with snakes! And swabs
parsing the glitter in the city's drains.

(Art that is easily understood)

Tampon of polity. Staunched, we rise up
guilty of dust. The state we're in. In one
fell swoop the glass falls in a freezing rain.
We have brought down an alphabet of cranes.

(Sonnet: Sonata)

*lleluia, alleluia. Sing along,
in the sound language, Thou, to everie one.*

Late in Time

Late in time, as we now are,
when polities of the *corpus* (planet)
ail on each other, in a general

collapse, there is yet *rue*
as our yearning over what
error we were, and that torn

cry of our gulled heart, recalling
a hue of light
or the first time we held

hands, morning after,
when the birds published us
to a passing world.

The sea is full of bottles.
It does not warrant this
pupa of prayer, without message,

to clutter some farther shore.
The great currents
convey their waters;

why bottle their waves?
And yet people will stand
to their isolate duties

on balconies at this,
the equinox,
and sing off the pages

of their imperilled lungs,
their hearts out, as birds
sing for the shifting

dawn, always somewhere
occurring. And the nations
of the dead do not matter

to the dead, or to the dying
world. If only the air was always
this clear. If only there had been

time, as the time kept singing,
as we now are, as we now
ail, as the world has ailed.

Landfall

Rain on the wing, streaming like anchovies
over fathoms of night. Descent
is tissue pressure: brow to the unlikely

double-glazing, the grease of dozing
there, scrap
dreams, the long amen of the engines.

It's a controlled fall on a dark
upwelling wanting
some noun of capacity—*Benguela*, say, *Agulhas* …

The laying-on of eyes:
black brine, with bloom storms under, and
down there the scintillate planktons, feather-

star cities of light.
Making landfall, then, this
slump on all that is

laid out, cold, the embroidered
cloths, etc., and there the showered
lamplight on the apron, and the moths.

None of this will last. Nor
day's pretty extinction, nor night's
resumption, our bright

autarchy—but the waste of sleep
wells up where sleep will, in widening
pores of the great tomorrow.

Now on this dark runway, lugged
down where the lights lie
bent in rising air —

the aurora of something at sea portending
itself, deceiving itself,
with a morse of tapers —

we are queued like grammar, wanting
an object sleep, and we'll get it:
sentenced, and the lights out.

Equator

We drowse in the perpetuum, eventually awed
by the human compress, our mass mutual intubation
at altitude, whether drugged or distressed: night

transit again, traversing the globe in a thin
nylon blanket, brittle with static. The long *Amen*
of the engines' breathing becomes our own.

Far below lie the fires of settlements, of which
these dreams, sliding on the window—a suddening
to mind, of the just-as-far past. I am vivid

among ghosts again, and again, like the loop
in the playlist, they come through the grass of a summer
in my teens, looking north to mountains,

and my love for you then is diffused through some
total I cannot explain, but is the sweet grass and the rock,
the duration of days across years, the compass

of a young heart high in ambition. The day is
red-lettered in the upper air, before the throne
up there, where the life is judged on these crossings.

Writing this, I know what it means to bless *all unawares*.
I watch my own film on the screen of closed eyes:
always the two women crossing the rising road, who

climb through the fence and walk on into Lesotho.
Not dreams, then, but waking reveries, never more
alert or alive, equally close to the past and to prophecy.

They answer the description of love with conviction, but
leave also the certainty that love is a question and not
its answer. It is easy to say we are so transported.

And yet this: though it is the platonic vision I am
vouchsafed at thirty-thousand feet, yet it remains
Eros who accompanies me through Passport Control.

For want of the body's earthing, I take an airport
coffee, and then stand outside in the season of another
hemisphere, all smelling different (ever the first impression),

and I feel as surely aroused as spiritually translated.
The elderflower and diesel of a northern summer, or
the flinty scent of winter light itself: I strike the first

match of the abstinent hours and smoke a cigarette
and am as free as I'll ever be, and each body is a story
in the sudden expectation of the arrived world.

So, later, when I leave my village, and the dawn due its dreaming,
I leave my poems at No. 8 across the piazza, whom I
loved with conviction and never hear of again, or see.

Talking About the Weather

~ *after Aristotle*

For poetry tends more to universals
than history's particulars, and yet what
comfort of that which cannot happen over.

Though grimly does. All night (it is
all night) the resurrected sea
makes landfall, pulping the dead boughs,

sowing hail against the step, and
taking the kitchen window with its
electric photograph. This is now

political, and as an imperilled people
so gather with all your bells to clamour,
scald mouths, preach planet to power.

Ever the common tongue, the
plaisant commonplace: under one
weather held in a single honour,

accounted none. Now does a single
swallow make a world of difference.
Black as a glove thrown down.

There is a path we have called Japan,
so lovely: and there the thrush tending
to dark and the dark wild almond.

3

The War of Makhanda

The history of the fourth war of resistance
begins with some resolution in the ordinal number:
a tally of bloodletting.

It lasted one day. The books have it outlined,
though we want for Makhanda's actual invocation
at the issue of Xhosa from the bush, north.

When the time came for running, the war
was runaway too. How those fleeing stopped
their wounds with plugs of grass, amazed

at what firearms could do, the remoteness
of murder, and the incapacitated took to the water
to lie there, breathing through reeds.

Every one of those wars involved a river,
the notched imperial littoral, and a great drove of cattle.
Thus we learn among aloes. War is economy

and it never stops and history is not over
for the hungry who chew on plugs of grass,
tightening the famine belt. The great death

of cattle is yet to come, and the failure of ancestors.
Brereton will go on to bloody Bristol.
Makhanda will drown

and appear in countless visitations of hope, passing
incognito across country, down the long years
of exile and underground, toyi-toyi

and sabotage, the Time of the Comrades, and stand
as an ancestor to address the inevitable
crowd. The cattle will thin in the roadside smoke

of winter fires. You will drive carefully
north, into the hinterland of it all, and write
this poem, and the War of Hintsa will still happen.

A Short Walk in the Zuurveld

1

In medias res: flourished cymbals.
Can there be welding one world? Land lies
felled in its falsehood, far as eye
can carry it. Rain sifts
as brass rice on the bridal ground.
Honey and spit.

2

We cannot go to ground, or past.
Ndlambe ups to damn and be
damned, the
aloes drip their myth in drizzle.
Pineapple lands, a country cut
whichway: choose ham or cicatrice or

3

barbered skull. Last shouts
in broken weather, kinds of homecoming,
none. She's walked the years'
bounds of her home fields, put
the handkerchief of smoke there.
By 'she': the ground gone over.

4

Banns, banned, bannered, it is conjugated,
chained by survey, trod
by rod, found finite among the scorched
earths of earth. Who is ever coming
to the rites under intervals of light?
Kingdom coming over the watershed.

5

How lovely is the seducer in the cloth
of gold, shot silks of accidental sky.
Be fortified in spirit or in stone, the gun-
loops frame the narrow gate:
traffic of small doves plies
there, gun-smoke monkeys

6

drift across the canopy of eye. Today
they squat diamonded in muss
flurrying about their closed canteen.
It has become goat country. It is bit
down, capillaried with staggers. The horned
god stays to the end.

7

Pan-congregants in white are gone wide to make
the Love Forage, who flock their yarn
on thorn, consider the nuptials thorough.
What matters, but that no bush burns?
Unhallowed ground. Under brazen
cloud, the astonished

8

chapels issue their dead,
ordnance of the word.
Feet washed in a clay slip.
Who stands third on the field of war?
Is this not one question you should ask
into the midst of things, why should there be

9

ever three, or goats, or kings, fuel for
that fiery furnace? Tales' trinities.
For the third time, sky golds
and waters. Has it so, history, that lets
blood like fields, the only dampened drought.
That it must be begun, endured, and run.

10

Third is ever after, as must always
be, some riddance, the billy, the kid.
It seems forever that the bride turns
back on bad weather, into the midst again.
Cymbal dwindles in pools of air. Quittance
there is none, but night.

11 *Coda*

Well-thumbed, hitched, hiked, ascended
the truckload throne of chicken feet, to lie
baled, out of the mire, all strutting done, so come
to power with immodest haste by night, now's
unending middle, to the vision
pent: ostrich surge in a pink electric flock.

Quagga Foal

~ *South African Museum*

1

Done to the life, this sleeping beauty
stands her ground, but her glazed stare
and our curiosities are coffined there.

2

The head is vast with project: *how to be.*
Massive cheek. Her mother's somewhere.
Neither's here nor now. We're what's left

3

to the telling of a former truth:
Of all my travils in Africa, yet
this was beautifullest to see —
hundreds of Quakers running in droves.

4

(A mission in the east at morning
two hundred years ago; where now
we drive past signs to *Eseljag*.)

5

The last, we heard, succumbed on concrete
in a German zoo. A botched job, too,
from the say-so: your panto donkey,

6

half-and-half, the wild ass aimed
at something tremendous, never
getting there. It fell between and there remains.

7

Antic creation that is our one end:
bestow on us our nucleic acids,
the family nose, our passage bones.

8

Bring us dugongs and ghost frogs, bats, black
widows, seagrass and lilies, kissing
cousins, mates, milk teeth, the company

9

of congeners and a common blood
shed and resumed. Bless we this donkey.
It has found its majority now

10

in the species of the dead. We are
scarce alive, we are the smallest dust,
and though the stats are stacked in strata

11
all against us, as a reckoning:
what wilderness! O, the zero-point-
one per cent within us and abroad

12
so seeming certain, which can yet hear
this foal in its vitrine calling for
milk still fail. And the beetles come.

Plovers

Announcing that degree of dark thorough,
though soon after the fall of dark, the kiewiets
blow bleating overhead, like angels over Egypt.
They tear the first page of night across.

And you yelp inwardly at their bidding, across
as many years as fields. If you think back
to the second train, Lights Out, the reek
of cinders and the shriek of steam, there

are those sad sirens, the plovers, the broken
country. For how long did they mean going
home? You could use them to date the depth
charge of first love, as precipitate as that

winter dusk, or the Eighties' States
of Emergency. In fact, one night fell as you
sat on the pavement in a blackout, waiting
for a lift, talking politics, and there

their black bells, ringing like writing, or
the lines inked out under the law. The city
under the arches of your ribs still kept
its firstborn love, and when the kiewiets

call still does. They were the radio under
your pillow, the Top Twenty, the troop carriers.
Their cries fell as soot in your hair, and
you will no more wash them out now than then.

Seventeen Depositions on Two Mechanical Breakdowns

~ Sekhukhuneland, 1986

1

High up, the dark was petro-smoke.
Smut mascara of burned wax, night
like a dump fire, and dust gusting.
Eels of ground fog flailing the wheels.

2

Like I was hurrying towards what I was hurrying
from, down-night, every fuse a treason.
Intermittent orange. Turned neither, nor.
Dashboard died like a belief in ghosts.

3

By my last lights I took in the outer night.
Owls came apart.
Old newspapers tore
up on the tar. Eyes shone two by two,

4

stood where the dark was washed away, conjured
the spirit kin, oh man,
dropped into the ditch of night.
Doppler shunts, and dog's breath blew in.

5

In the red hills of the chrome workings,
labour caged in sleep, as soot,
barren stars of spotlights were blazing a quiet.
The spark failed, and dark succeeded.

6

I was there at the electric end, at the bridge
too far. Zero traffic. Insects wung the car.
I heard what I had heard all along, some
song of a copper brush wrung wrong.

7

The river slept soaped with Sunlight,
subtracted for metals upriver and down.
It went without saying.
Engine tutted in its quiet. A lovers' night

8

on low ground. Heat prowling and a hundred
fires constellating as many hills—wasn't
so bad to have died right then.
Leaned there on the air and waited.

9

So I was, say,
fifty metres into Sekhukhuneland,
dogs crooning from here to the equator,
enough light to see the wild pigs by.

10

Believe my eyes, he crept over the bridge
boiling his radiator for a flue of stars.
Pitied me, God bless, and took me up,
with our backs to his weekdays,

11

the coal he mined, its stations burning
up aeons in the maize.
His tyres boiled on gravel in his dark yard,
ferrous gravel, ring to it, and there his wife

12

stood to the moonlight, only dreaming
herself in our steam, in a pearl
nylon skirt, remember that, and brought
water in a gourd, for God's sake.

13

And there was more electricity
under the hood than across all the hills. Still
she stood lucent as Lot's Wife in nylon, nothing
besides, in the affidavit of the moon.

14

Filled the radiator in conclave by the scrap
light of celestial bodies, pointing with cigarettes.
Some children came to the door of the dream,
adding their eyes to the sum of the available.

15

This is the thing about memory. My own
dead car cools abandoned under a tarp of sky,
stars waiting in its windows,
passenger stars, sleeping on the laps of stars,

16

and for how long, and how it was got going
I know not now. Across the years, the hills,
the river, I am looking back only at that
column of unimpassioned light

17

by which we operate, transplanting
water, clear for rust, stars in a gourd,
that eucharist on magnetite gravel.
The common prayer.

Night Transit

~ Transvaal, c. 1989

It's just one passenger
and one postilion in
the taxi, on the run
crossing KwaNdebele.

The state we're in. The sun
comes in at Ntwane, sets
at Dennilton in dust.
His AK-47

scuds to the floor. We touch
one-sixty. Brotherly
love; songs of the earth lie
in the wheels, sweet porridge

on the night air. The lights
of Philadelphia go
down in the back window.
Our Hi-Ace intercepts

a slow VW
tramp-steaming to the south.
Heave to and board beneath
stars' flares. This is a new

order out of the old.
This is the remembered
future to be endured
as love again, to hold

close, sharing the common
blanket, sharing shoulders.
Here where all are elders,
breathing the one carbon

monoxide through the floor.
We cross the Winterveld
to Monday. Work. This world
the one sleep wakes us for.

And My Heart, Maputo

Because intimacy is reaching
the same conclusion,
there's more to love than going
through the motions, inept
in sweat, eeling around
on hot nights, bats yelping like puppies.
You'll know something
staggering the heart in its separate stride.
Nights almost pass while the bay
fails again, the pipes chafe, the sewers
smirch the air and we climb
up through leagues of breath but never
breach, and somehow sleep.

Tropic lust, mealy as the air.
There's more love in chivvying
the urinous filament of water
falling wide, washing, or taking you
by your arm into an oven shade
to water you, make you smile.
How wide is the Avenida Karl Marx?
You said as wide as the world gone
round at the equator. Too brilliant
for shadow, light scalds
even the obverse. Nothing
swoons like a heart felled
on its parade. I, too,

suffer my metabolic engines to burn
backwards at over 37 degrees.
Air tastes like bathwater.

We wade into each other.
We should have let our photograph
be taken at the gardens, if only
to look into the pupil of so long ago,
the hot steel Seventies
camera, its cool paper future.
Believe me, even now
your heart squirts in the brine
bay of my body, our squids
in the same conclusion of ink.

To the East

Driving into dawn, the children sleeping,
all's pointed east. The elder sacrament:
light might yet be your subject. Now it stalls
on contact, skin. Whatever season holds

you in its debt—once leaving rain in vines,
once pollen billowing on tar—the road
refuses understanding, passing through
all it exists to conjugate. The dead

are strewn just out of town, in recent ground
cut for a mortal suburb. At the gates:
sufficient shade to wait, but there's no bus.
You (cornflakes, *dammit, wine*) look east where crows

writhe in their flak-jackets, on rising air
at the adjacent dump always on fire.

To the West

~ *vir J. H.*

Foundered on tenebrous ground, you scarcely
see: but the land's flat-lined, farming shadow.
Out into the bloated sea the gaze
sails to its failure, and the waves stink

of a cold-water crop, tonnages of krill.
A factory sauces the sunburnt air. Wheat
comes dark, born into stubble, and the blue
crush of shell grinds out the landfall, which is all

you make. Perhaps a battleship or battery waits.
What is God got in all these towns named Peace?
Annihilation, doom come as heaven:
slap of a sail against a steel tube all

day long. *Dink! Dink!* The long lagoon shot pink
under wined clouds, seething with thumbnail crabs.

Witwatersrand

Ceremony of smuts and jacaranda, fanfare
of a traffic brazen in the leaded dust. Stand
before the storm's iconostasis when it comes:
the god's got up in gold that sweat has rusted.

Land is always rising, leavened of what? The light
bent in atmospheric clutter and resumed
as shone grass, successions of groundwater begun,
begun again. Winter ascended into heaven.

Beyond the noose of motorway, where kennels vie
with nurseries, occasional vultures tow the skies.
The ground is fallen in, with its unlucky apes
returned in lime. So housing projects multiply

and haven't time, because the fucking rain, *O*
come on now. The townships. Planes hurry up.

Old Photographs, or, the Developed Eye

Transects of the one light. The emporia
stow them in shoeboxes, in which cardboard
chantries prayers might be shuffled through. This
is the empire of the dead. The wind grinds

out its one tune taught of the Atlantic,
sauced with light. Day fattens against the odds.
What is breast-pocketed, or who? 'John Brown,
Accra, 1952.' In the stern

he towers, of that pontoon in which you will
be seen to shore. Down there his arms are flung
abroad. It is now. Is his top hat more
to be trusted, or the very end? Look,

you take the continent like its photograph;
light cumulates there, light throws you back.

On Trying to Sleep at Kareedouw

Summer night, creosoted, the stars there
tarred, the owl flung up out over
polity of the lumber-yard, suburbs of timber,

some sense of the sad, unvisited hills,
massifs of grit, fossil, ash. This late
stage. Enter by the tired eye, that had torn

up the ribbon of its invented road, gone
AWOL of itself, seen the moon lobbed
across successive skies and die in one.

Had this been prayer, it would have been
hapless as prayer must be, rightly reckoned.
The car was on its knees, you could say that

and tell no more lie than speech just must.
The cafés are closed, their stock is yesterday,
wrought stars, streetlights. Corpuscular

quaking, as the blood's sent forward. How
to lug it back and sleep? The engine throws
the wet penumbra of its furnace, seethes

in what has scorched, the favours of bugs.
Does the god wait even at this doomed
cash-and-carry, where the stars are parked,

and it's too rumorously quiet, the choral
dogs, the police arriving
in lights? That's three a.m. The body's

mired in sponge of the assembled
miles, and the offending party shakes the air
like a drunk, its music done like blood

down the distance of your ear. Those cinereal
hills incapable of echo. There's but the hot
key, hot air. There's putting more behind.

4

Cutting

It is my best knife and my favourite.
The knife of my hand.

It is the knife he gave to me
and I paid so that it would not come between us.

Now it has come between us
and I remember him by it who never thought
he would be remembered by a knife
alloyed with so much carbon
it grows a lichen of oxide like a stone.

I chop mint and parsley
and he is dead whom I loved.

Skies

~ *in memoriam SFW*

Radiant granite, Atlantic evening:
my daughter and her beloved implicate
their hands by counterpointing fingertips
to make that mirror of the world they are.
Let set the sun! Let slip the knots of knuckles!
It's love, and drawn in charcoal on a sky
out of this world: *passion-fruit cordial,*
clouds of smashed asbestos. I owe you your
barley-water, dry-white-wine, habitual
skies. I have seen even that flat, shattered
chalk, the perished balloon you wagered
everything on. You are not wrong, just dead.
The cormorants whittle each other's necks
to love-spoons. Planets begin their thing.

Under the Loquat

He had that majority under the loquat,
rain falling like a god in gold, the breakthrough
sun, and the spin on things, tar growing a fur.
Loitered there looking into the intenser
day, as kids emerged along the road again
in slops and polyester, kissing sugar.
How sober could he be in a white-wine rain?
Let's say he showed a surplus. It matters not
of what. But that she called from France was extra.
They spoke in electricity. He reached up
and took a loquat from the god-sodden bough,
found it furred like a cat's tongue, with a cat's brass
scent of advent, a litter of stones within.
All of it then more; and more years ago now.

Tabernacle

You laid me between you and you
held my breath. Day spread its sail
over us, our shroud shone. We lay
transfigured and yet world went on.

You held my breath. Was it always?
Certainly you held me and you
let me go. Sunlight wrote shadows
on canvas overhead. A beetle fell.

You drew your sheet back like morning.
That was where I came in.
World droned in daylight, world
without end. Air was burning

on your breath, as if with paraffin.
I lay in that canvas lung, that lit
air breathed me in. You drew
your sheet back as breath and world fell in.

I am remembered by you
as I was when. Beetle and shadow
prosper in sunlight. Write them then.
You hold my breath. Is it again?

Lie me between you and you
hold my breath. Draw your sheet
back and breathe me in,
hold me. And hold me when.

Mercurial Day

~ *for MB*

The cloud is clearing the mountain
with a soft insistence upon fact:
this mass of rock and time given
so gently, so simply. It could be
asking our *nunc dimittis* of the world
as it is. Mine eyes have seen.

What of this so-ordinary miracle,
patient as a Chinese watercolour,
but that it is how you came
so simply, perhaps not gently,
into my life, that became ours?
It is the way of being.

Let us tell the truth. We have made
love as the wind to the mountain,
rubbing God into existence. Night
after night the wind was quarrying
the scream of stone. *Dio!* I stood
at your window and looked into it.

I will tell you what I found:
to lay things bare might mean
first to flay them, so the wind wants
truth of the rock, rock of the wind.
I saw that, and that the wind had gentled
of a sudden and the stone stayed,

and though the wind is winning the war
of love, it is taking forever.
We have all the time in the world.
It is Wednesday morning and the clouds—
just clods of fog—dissolve.
Breath on a window.

Trucks are shunting groceries into the maw
of commerce under apartment 108,
a wasp drifts over the drifting
rotors of the air-con on the roof,
and suburban trees are cropping light,
patient under the patient immensities.

In fact—the fact of time—there is nothing
patient. Things just are,
nor suffer, nor greet.
It is we who die so soon who find
ourselves impatient as the wind, we
who suffer our patience to marvel

at stone or sun, their unfailing
entailed regard, so quietly shining
to one another it looks like passion.
And is a kind, and a kind of kindness:
just being there, collateral, with one
another on another Wednesday morning.

North Ship

I lie in bed some nights and think *Fuck it,*
for a lark, in ten minutes I could be out
of here and on the freeway bridge, and flag
down a northering truck, and I feel all
its momentum bulge in me as pregnant
as the impressive pause between its gears.
Something of that snarl, too, cutting both ways
for and against my going. Why don't I then?

Cosy I find the night-lit cab, gazing
down on traffic, the road-marks swimming up
to me like sperm, the N1 issuing
itself anew, anew, anew. And you,
whoever you may be, yet keep me true,
if that's not going, but to be going to.

Llanelieu

But a depot of lucid air,
deconsecrated, bat-shat, still
holy with years and holy, too,

the head of any valley. Here
a loud, lit silence in the round,
this Celtic precinct of the dead,

toppled stones and a flogging yew,
where immemorial sheep still mow
the parish to its common ground.

The bones of Price and Gwynne now list
in a soil sea. Nobody yet
settled a farther shore, unless

shepherds be counted, or their kin
who cast for souls on the black hill
at Llanthony. Of men, amen:

none stay, as none can, but some sense
of having been. God's own baleen,
ridges of winter conifers,

the palisades of marcher barons,
assert the watershed. From there
they state the facts. Shadows broadcast

long over damp valleys. A fox
crosses from one to another dark.
Is this the taper of the sun

kindling a dark church, doing here
the work of red? Somehow aghast
we lay together in the wards

of love in a bed of snow here,
entering the lists of thrown bones.
Once in summer on a green grave.

You taught me all I then forgot
of love in a long dying, but
there is always here. The church, shut,

still stands, and I have it engraved
here with my hand, and yours where once
you held it, then over my mouth

so as not to raise the wrack dead
on our glad day, or bury us
in snow on one another. The road

there climbs in dark woods and in rain
gilded in sodium light as far
as streetlamps straggle out of town;

I am coming back to here again,
marching against the dark come down
to meet me on a glacial tar,

and have come far, and far from you
this way, carrying my own bed,
as I must lie on at Llanelieu.

5

Last Things

This transit of the whole self tending
al estero, which is also home. The last
hour on this earth, a last look round
the freeway north. We pause to pay

our tolls and sort our baggage out.
Ciao bella. From the back seat I
let what little light fall in to digitise.
I make an image of a clan of trees:

it's black and white, passed back
down decades of the common eye,
a bulletin of departure, which is to say
memorial. And farms slide by.

That this should be last things.
A sequence of lane changes, Sat-nav,
the broad hips of the Po.
Later the lug of take-off, concrete

cast on the word 'soil', as you think it,
dykes of degraded snow, the
runway cleared, and down below
the months become a postcard sent yourself.

The Common

Had that solstice cold within begun
its careful damage? Nothing for granted
is what it took. It was that without
which there is no staggering the soul

in compulsory darkness, tin light,
mornings to be heard across themselves
end to end, and, at dusk, dusk putting
hatchling lights into the river. Walking

clamped to the cold, as cold year to year,
kicking through the rotted shadows,
spores of ice in a fog falling
all across the common, day led

the way home, to the put lights in the night
day drew. That day was the shortest
cut across the common, through
the longing fog falling for the trees.

World Enough

Sleep then. Let life the lullaby
compose you. Close your eyes.
Nail down their lids, heavy as need
six good men to heave.

New worlds discover you, who were
world enough to us awake.
Day breaks and breaks on the bone shore
doves call you to.

Uncompassed latitudes engrave
your map of nonsense. Leave.
On linens of your raft adrift
light out for salvage.

Foundling, sleep. Let the sad house you
were brought up to now sleep.
Let fall your windings wrung of the one
brine bone grew in.

Lay yourself down on that threshold
ledge and be brought in.
Doves wash you while a far fridge
stays singing its one thing.

Doves gather in your rafters, roost
in your bone waves broken;
they fledge your spread arms. The vacuum
grieves in each room going.

Bees furl under your ribs and burn
unfurling in a chimney.
Learn of their dark devising how
must needs be not why.

Good earth takes to it your treasure
only loaned to us. Sand
on which sea broke is broken, your
clay tongue turns clay.

Now sleep. Dream not, but be dreamed down
years, as roots are dreamed of trees.
You are remembered, who to light
brought eyes that lowered ours.

Light prospers where your eyes become
coin now, your skin burns out.
You are slept into light. Surely
sleep then. Let life go by.

Little Poem of the Hare and the Stars

Under an astonishment of stars,
as a hare leaves its form, so
stood the matter: desire, of yours—

and to the hare the stars have a cindery
scent, and to the hare the nethers
of vine and hummock are as desire.

Night: cinders and plain earth.
All the bright shiners and the tales
told on them. The matter stood

as you before the judge that's Time.
There are the Sisters and the Hunter's Dog.
The hare is started

between two desires and will be run
down—as desire goes—to ground.
The matter that stood then lay

between desire and desire, of yours—
finding its form forever, an instant
in which the zodiac was dropped

like a cigarette or an expensive brooch
at the roots of what grew there
and Time was astonished with stars.

The Once

The road remembered him and he drove down
his lights as had a leaping hare, its eyes
tossing their coins in the compassing night,
road-signs prophesying. Then in the dark

conclave of that hour before dawn bleaches
land and sky and thought, and the road between,
he was convinced of her, across the years
his passenger, to whom he turned and laid

siege there, and saw for Troy in dismal
dashboard light. It was another sleeping
against the glazed night where stars and diesel
slid. All the same, he told her that he loved

her by his tucking back her hair. Then wept
the once, and in the rear-view watched day break.

Acknowledgements and Permissions

Thanks are due to the editors of the following journals and anthologies where versions of some of these poems first appeared: *The London Magazine, The Rialto, Denver Quarterly, The Hopkins Review, TEXT, Tremble, New Contrast, New Coin, Blue Earth Review* and *Stanzas*.

The author is deeply grateful to Hanien Conradie for the cover and interleaving artwork.

P. R. Anderson

Notes on Epigraphs and Quotations

Phrases, epigraphs and quotations have been used, sometimes with and sometimes without acknowledgement.

Page 14

When I grew to about thirteen years of age . . . I was contrited under a sense of power and love.

— Sarah Lynes Grubb (1773–1832), *Quaker Faith and Practice* 5ed (London: Britain Yearly Meeting of Religious Society of Friends, 2014) chapter 28, 28.04

Page 21

Months have passed, each one filled with foreboding and silence. Now disasters are flowing together into a delta that has no name, and will only be given one by geographers, who will come later, much later.

— John Berger , 'A Place Weeping', *The Threepenny Review*, Summer 2009

Page 23

Fahrkarte bis zur Endstation is German for 'Tickets to the last station'—Guderian's hallmark exhortation to his advancing troops in Blitzkrieg. (Guderian was the iconically successful general of Blitzkrieg. His fortunes foundered just short of Moscow, his furthest advance being to Tolstoy's estate at Yasnaya Polyana.)

Page 23

we are all held in a single honour

Homer. 1955. *Iliad*. London : New York : Dent; Dutton. Book 9. 318-320.

Page 27

Carduelis carduelis (*Fringilla carduelis*. Linn. 1758).

The original Linnaean taxonomic binomial.

Page 38

Tell el-Amarna, New Kingdom is an extensive Egyptian archaeological site of the ruins and tombs of the city of Akhetaton.

Page 48

Umnyele is isiXhosa for the Milky Way.

Page 50

O ye religious, discountenance every one among you who shall pretend to despise Art and Science!

—William Blake, 'Jerusalem'

Page 66

Of all my travils in Africa, yet
this was beautifullest to see —
hundreds of Quakers running in droves.

From the unpublished diary of George Barker, South African Library, Cape Town

Printed in the United States
by Baker & Taylor Publisher Services